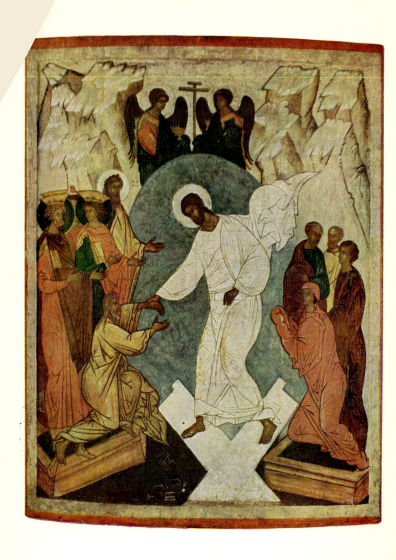

Reinhold Lange

THE RESURRECTION

AUREL BONGERS RECKLINGHAUSEN
Distributed by Universal-Tandem Publishing Co. Ltd., London

PICTORIAL LIBRARY of EASTERN CHURCH ART

Vol. 16

Translated from the German by
Hans Hermann Rosenwald

Title page: Anastasis-Russian icon, beginning of the 16th century

© 1967 Aurel Bongers Publishers, Recklinghausen
Original edition: »Die Auferstehung«
Manufactured by Graphic Art Society Aurel Bongers, Recklinghausen

Printed in West Germany

Among the many pictures that grace the walls and the iconastases of Byzantine churches, the portrayal of the descent of Christ to Hell is one of the most significant, liturgically speaking. The portrayal concretizes the doctrine of salvation, the Resurrection of Christ. It therefore is accompanied by the words ANASTASIS.

At first glance the pictorialization of the Resurrection by means of the descent to Hell may appear strange. No less strange might be that the portrayal of this event of which the New Testament has nothing concrete to say became the festival icon of Easter, the highest orthodox holiday. In fact, the significance of the portrayal is even more astounding as we realize that the descent to Hell has played but a minor part in Western art; after all, ever since the eleventh century the West depicted the Resurrection of the Lord *from the grave*, and this type of pictorialization became a consistent and integral part of Western iconography from the beginning via Schongauer, Grunewald up to Rembrandt.

Eastern theology, however, would not allow the portrayal of Christ's Resurrection from the grave since no witnesses were in existence. This does not mean, however, that the descent to Hell alone made the realization of the Resurrection acceptable, and the descent to Hell is neither the only nor the earliest pictorial formulation of the Easter event. We ignore such portrayals that make reference to the Resurrection without communicating any of the "historical" circumstances such as the Jonah scenes of catacombs and sarcophagi, the youth in the fiery furnace, or Daniel in the lions' den. The guardians under the triumphant cross — in the plastic art of the sarcophagi of the fourth century — represent the event in symbolically abbreviated form. Additionally, another portrayal became popular from the third century on, a genuine "historical" picture at least in the sense of the early Christians: the three women at the grave. They approach the open grave in which the linen cloths are visible and "the napkin that was about His head, not lying with the linen cloths but wrapped together in a place by itself." (John 20, 7). The angel explains the miracle to the terrified Marys. This pictorial form remained valid up to the late Byzantine period, and enlarged festival cycles frequently show the three Marys at the grave together with the descent to Hell. One can understand that the form could not attain the rank of a festival icon because the chief figure, Christ Himself, is not represented. The theme is not so much the Resurrection as the *proof* that He was resurrected, and one can read little from it as regards the doctrines associated with the Resurrection of the Lord. No doubt this was found to be a major deficiency and favored a pictorial form that would be more to the point and closer to the doctrine of salvation. In Byzantium the decision was made in favor of the descent of Christ to Hades.

Such a decision, in reality the result of a development, is well founded in history and theology. However, one must adjudicate it from two viewpoints: first, how could it happen that a semi-apocryphal doctrine was elevated to an official festival representation, and secondly, in what way does the portrayal of the descent to Hades live up to its task, the representation of

Christ's Resurrection? The questions cannot be answered separately.

As has been stated many times, the idea of the descent of God or of heroes to Hades is of ancient Oriental origin (Ischtar, Tammuz, Isis, Orpheus, Hercules, etc.). The idea, strange to Judaism, was particularly cultivated in the syncretistic associations of late Antiquity. Its adaptation by Christianity probably took place in Antiochia or, at any rate, in Syria and Palestine. In the second century all of Christianity knew the myth of Christ's descent to Hell even though it was not everywhere accepted without questioning. It is also noteworthy that none of the writings dealing with the *descensus ad inferos* became part of the canon of the New Testament. However, the doctrine seemed acceptable and its protagonists had no difficulty in proving its truthfulness.

What is the core of this doctrine? Christ's soul, after He is buried, descends to Hades, destroys the portals of the underworld, proclaims the Gospel to the Just of the old Covenant and accompanies them to Paradise — with Adam and Eve at the helm, a new *psychopompos*. Thus the promise to David is fulfilled (Psalm 30, 3): "Lord, thou hast brought up my soul from the grave"; (Psalm 107): "For He hath broken the gates of brass and cut the bars of iron in sunder." And St. Peter on Pentecost had proclaimed the certitude that the promise had been fulfilled. Beyond that, in I Peter he speaks of the Gospel "preached also to them that are dead." And Paul in Hebrew II speaks of the victory over death and the redemption of the children of Israel. In the Letter to the Ephesians (4, 8—9) a similar thought appears: "When He ascended up on high He led captivity captive," and "Now that He ascended, what is to be that He also descended first into the lower parts of the earth?" and in the revelation of St. John we read similarly.

The Resurrection of Christ is guaranty for the Resurrection of the dead. In First Corinthians (15, 13) it says: "But if there be no Resurrection of the dead, then is Christ not risen," and St. Matthew (27) writes with absoluteness that: "The graves were opened; and many bodies of the saints which slept arose, and came out of the graves after His Resurrection, and went into the holy city and appeared unto many." Thus the word of Ezekiel (37) was fulfilled: "Behold I will open your graves and cause you to come up out of your graves and bring you into the land of Israel." The testimony of St. Matthew could be considered proof that Christ's salvation had been performed on the dead. This thought was to attain great significance for the young church.

If the fulfillment of the prophecies of the Old Testament had any value at all, the doctrine of the descent of the Son of God to the Just of the old Covenant, the redemption of Adam by Christ and the new Adam were particularly apt to demonstrate the inescapable connection of the teachings of the Old Testament and the doctrine of Christendom. At the same time the culmination of the old Covenant and its succession by Christ were thereby demonstrated. Both thoughts played an eminent role in the apologetics of early Christianity. In his "Dialog with the Jew Tryphon" (150—155) Justin comments on the descent of

Christ to Hades and of the redemption of the Just because he wants to clarify to the Jews that they must not disapprove of Christ as the true Messiah by referring to the prophets of the Old Testament: for the Gospel was proclaimed and they are saved by Jesus.

Not much later Irenaeus speaks of a presbyter who preached on the *descensus ad inferos*. Here, too, the intention was polemics, for Irenaeus attempted to speak against Gnosticism which in part tended to give up the Old Testament. Irenaeus adds that the preaching presbyter had acquired his knowledge from disciples of the apostles: by that addition he attempted to free the presbyter of the suspicion of being a heretic.

Even though the *descensus* of Christ is not part of the New Testament it was made believable and a good reconstruction attained by a series of quotations, and the doctrine was indeed useful in opposition to the enemies of Christianity; it was, in other words, useful in the disputations with Jews and in those with heretics. And it did not appear repulsive either to the heathen who, through Orpheus and Hercules, were well acquainted with the basic thought.

A sermon on the *descensus ad inferos* could scarcely ignore the "historical" illustration of the event. As early as in the second century there were no doubt detailed stories in circulation which dealt with these events. They are not preserved. The later versions of these stories are found in apocryphal writings, not taught though read. Their popularity was thereby not reduced, as is known from the later church fathers. Not even the fact that the descent to Hell was one of the last dogmatic statements that found admission to the *symbolum* of the old church detracted from its popularity.

The *Epistola Apostolorum* from Asia Minor or Egypt contain a narration of the *descensus,* and *The Shepherd of Hermas* speaks of a *descensus* of the apostle and the teachers. In the fourth century Ephrem the Syrian discusses the theme in his *Carmina Nisibena* and gives it poetic strength through his considerable artistic spontaneity. In the middle of that century Cyril of Jerusalem says: "He went to the Underworld so as to redeem the Just. Would you want that the living, most of whom are not pious, would benefit from His grace while those who since Adam were encased would not be set free? Isaiah the prophet with loud voice has proclaimed so much about Him: would you not want that the King should go down and redeem His herald? David was there, Samuel, all the prophets and even John . . . would you not want that He descend to Hell and redeem such men?" In such words Cyril tries to discredit those who were still doubtful. And in about 400 Synesios of Cyrene writes his hymns in the Dorian dialect. In one of them he gives artistic expression to Christ's descent to Hell. Finally, the recently rediscovered apocryphal revelation of St. Bartholemew contains the *descensus.*

At the beginning of the fifth century the Gospel of Nicodemus was penned. In its width and graphic artistry it combines all earlier representations and outdoes them all. The second part of this Gospel entitled *Descensus Christi ad inferos* is the basis for literary and pictorial portrayals of later periods. The doctrine of the descent to Hell was assured a definite place in the liturgy through the Easter hymns of the Greek church, and the liturgical position of the doctrine became the essential prerequisite for all pictorial renditions of the theme.

Just as is the case with so many themes of Christian art here, too, pictorial rendition succeeded the literary. That these pictorializations came late is scarcely astonishing in view of the controversial origin of the theme; yet that origin is scarcely the sole reason for the retardation.

The Nicodemus Gospel describes several events which, to be sure, lead to a definite climax; however, the climax is not completely in accordance with the significance of the event. The essential thought embraces three aspects: first, the proclamation of the Gospel to the ancestors, which is particularly stressed in the Peter epistle; secondly, the victory over Hades, or the devil, which is the real dramatic climax, and, thirdly, the redemption of the Just. The limitation to one of these aspects would in no case do justice to the significance of the event in pictorial representation. Therefore the artists had the task of blending three customary types of traditional iconography into one: firstly, Christ the teacher with the scrolls in His hand as He was represented in the meeting of the Apostles in the catacombs; secondly, Christ the victor, a motive of the victor over the dragon that since Constantine the Great was accepted in iconography and which was transferred to Christ ever since the fifth century (examples are in Ravenna, for instance); and thirdly, Christ the miracle performer — here the awakening of Lazarus could be used as prototype.

In other words, noone could do justice to the theme in one single rendition. One had to compile several elements which from the outset were, pictorially speaking, not logically connected. This is the reason why within the Byzantine pictorial canon, the descent to Hell remained one of the least constant compositions. It is so variable that even though the prototype is scarcely altered, one augments or reduces the number of persons; beyond that, the composition itself is erratic, developing ever new formulations. Though some of the latter had their motivation in varying artistic approaches, there were also tendencies to emphasize certain ideas by rendering them more prominent than others. The artists had the choice between dramatic action or a representative passivity. To be sure, the theme offered not just problems but also potentialities. It seems that all possibilities were utilized and that difficulties gave ever new impulses to the inventive powers of creative artists.

We know neither time nor place when the first artist dared to undertake the portrayal of this theme. One may conjecture that he, whoever he was, dealt not with a mural in a church but with a little piece of parchment of book page size, for book illumination gave more freedom to the painters than did anything monumental. Nor was book illustration adjudicated in terms of the severe criteria of Byzantine iconology. Portrayals that in murals would have been provocative, could go unchallenged in book illumination for these books were accessible to but small circles of

Anastasis · Fresco, middle of the 9th century

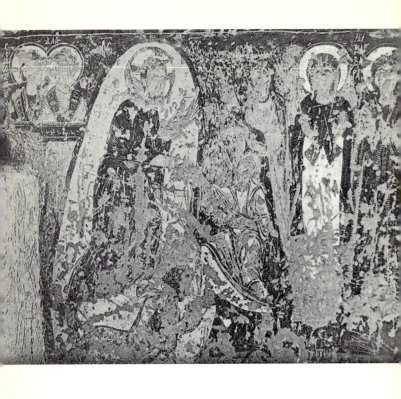

Anastasis · Fresco, middle of the 10the century

book owners. The painter's access to the murals of churches, on the other hand, was made possible only when a controversial belief was approved of as a dogma. There is sufficient reason, then, to assume that the portrayal of the *descensus* was initiated in book illumination. In fact the theme remained the favorite subject for miniaturists and is invariably present in the illustrations of the Psalter.

Documents preserved start in ca. 700 — strangely enough not in book illumination which incidentally is sparsely represented at that time. At any rate, what we possess are scarcely the earliest examples, an assumption further confirmed by *two* basic types obviously representing two different localities.

The first type comes from Syria and Palästine and first appears in miniatures. Three little Niello portrayals demonstrate the development of two hundred years. The oldest is from the collection Fieschi-Morgan (New York Metropolitan Museum) and shows all essential elements later found in mature compositions (see page 16). In an oblong area a large figure of Christ steps toward the right where we see the small figures of the ancestors. Christ takes the hand of Adam while Eve lifts her hands in prayer. The grip of Adam's wrist by the Resurrected symbolizes salvation and the new Adam, Christ, leads the saved old Adam from Hades to Paradise. In the upper left corner we see, raised from a sarcophagus, the busts of two kings with Byzantine crowns: David, singer of Psalms, and Solomon. Even though the Nicodemus gospel mentions only David, we see both kings as on almost all other portrayals. At Christ's feet we see a small figure clothed with a loin cloth, the defeated Hades. He grabs with one hand at Christ's foot and tries to stop Him. In the upper right corner one sees two small rectangles representing the broken doors to Hell. Neither kings nor doors are organically integrated into the composition but are like symbols added to complete the scenery.

Not much later is the origin of the small Niello cross in the church of Vicopisano (see page 17). It is Eastern art from the first part of the eighth century. Though in details not much different from our previous example, it is more compact. Rays emanate from Christ's figure. One of the doors has been moved from the upper right corner to the lower left. It is, so to speak, on the way to the place in which these doors are seen from the ninth century on: at Christ's feet. A third portrayal, on a trip-

tych in Tiflis, though crude is compositionally more highly developed (see page 18). The three main figures are of almost like size. At the feet of Christ three doorwings are ordered so that one obtains the impression that hte Lord goes through them. Below Adam we see a sarcophagus. There is no fi-

Anastasis
Niello Tableau, ca. 700

16

gure of Hades. Christ carries in His left hand the scroll, a symbol that the gospel is proclaimed to the dead. For the first ime the inscription H ANACTACIC appears so that there is no doubt: the portrayal is the Easter event. The *descensus* had survived iconoclasm, it had become the official icon of the highest holiday of the church.

A little enamel plate (see page 19) from Georgia exhibits one considerable change: the doorwings are at the feet of Christ. A certain development is thereby concluded (in the tenth century), but soon there is a search for new ideas and inspirations. However, let us first glance at the second group of the earlier portrayals of the anastasis.

From the beginning of the eighth century we find in Rome three *descensus* frescoes deviating from the Syrian-Palestinian type. They originated during the pontificate of John VII. Since he was a Greek it is highly probable that we are here faced with a type from Constantinople which in Byzantium itself is no longer traceable. There are two frescoes in Santa Maria Antiqua (see page 25) and on the way to the platform of the Palatine and a mosaic in the prayer hall of John VII, the latter, however, preserved only in a copy.

Anastasis
Silver cross (segment), 1st half of
the 8th century

17

Anastasis · Nielloenkolpion, 9th century

In all three compositions Christ, surrounded by an oval *mandorla*, steps from left to right. The kings are absent but in the example of Santa Maria Antiqua we do see mummies in one fresco. On the other Eve is absent. On both frescoes, just as we have seen before, Hades grabs for Adam's feet. Christ does not form the center of the composition but is shown vis-à-vis Adam.

This form did not last long in Rome or in Byzantium, and the Roman documents prove that in the ninth century the type from Syria and Palestine had prevailed. A mosaic fragment from the Zeno chapel in S. Prassede has Christ as central figure turning toward the right side. The *mandorla* of the old Roman tradition is preserved, but now there is the addition of an angel. During the pontificate of Leo IV, i. e., in the middle of the ninth century, the anastasis in S. Clemente originated (see page 13). It also shows Christ turned toward the right. On another portrayal in the same church Christ has a cross staff. Adam comes forward from the Underworld surrounded by flames. A little brown figure of Hades grabs at his foot. Eve is absent, perhaps she disappeared together with the right part of the fresco.

Roman frescoes of the ninth century also served as model for similar compositions in Müstair and Cimitile. The portrayal of the anastasis has now come to its temporary conclusion in the West. Sporadically the theme appears in book illumination (Cotton Psalter, eleventh century) and in crafts (shrine of Farfa,

Anastasis
Enamel plate, 1st half of the
10th century

eleventh century). In mural painting it becomes gradually popular again in the twelfth century (Tavant, Touraine.) After 843,
the end of iconoclasm, the Syrian-Palestinian type becomes the
rule also in Byzantium, at least in mural painting. Examples of
the ninth and tenth centuries are found among the frescoes of
Cappadocian cave monasteries. The anastasis of Chapel 6 of
Göreme, the church of Keledjlar, the Theotokos chapel and others
have in common that Christ is turned toward the right; they
also show the *mandorla* and the kings, in part as demi-figures, in
the sarcophagus.

In the Theotokos chapel, as is seen on page 14, Hades grabs
after Adam's foot. In the older church of Toqale (tenth century) the anastasis is shown next to the women at the grave but
so that the empty grave, as is seen on page 24, belongs to both
portrayals. In that manner one has the impression that Christ
leaves the grave in order to complete His salvation of the dead.
Behind Christ over His grave there are two kings. again figures
in a sarcophagus. As seen on page 21, the composition is enlarged
in the Barbara church of Soghanli (ca. 1000); here we see four
persons resurrected from the grave with an inscription: I NEKPY
EKTON MNHMATON ANICTANTO, which reminds us of
St. Matthew. Here, too, Hades reaches out for Adam's foot;
Christ does not hold the scroll but the cross staff.

In contrast to murals which are fairly unified up to the
beginning eleventh century, book illumination, particularly in
the ninth century, offers an abundance of variations which make
us aware of the potential of *descensus* portrayals. Particularly

Anastasis · Fresco, ca. 1000

Anastasis · Miniature, 9th century

in the Psalter Codices do we find highly diversified compositions. Since the idea of salvation from death plays a great role in Psalms, David was easily regarded the personification of mankind seeking salvation. The Chludov Psalter of Moscow, exhibiting four different types of anastasis and representing one of the most significant examples of book illuminations of the ninth century, seems to have almost no connection whatsoever with mural paintings of that time and in several details is much closer to early Roman compositions, that is, early Constantinople types. In part the direction toward the left is preserved; kings and gates to Hell are absent. In one miniature (see page 26) Christ is seen on the head of a gigantic Hades who is seated facing the onlooker. Christ with His left hand has embraced Adam's wrist, at His right Eve lifts her arms toward the Lord. And the illustration of Psalm 67 (see page 28) uses a scheme that found treatment in murals much later: Christ steps upward holding Adam by the wrist. He looks back at him in a scene which is laid over the gigantic figure of the defeated Hades who seems to push downward, in an audacious shortening, into the lowest part of the icon. No less extraordinary is the anastasis in the Parisian Psalter fragment (see page 22) from the ninth century. In an illustration of Psalm 106 we find here a portrayal of Christ between Adam and Eve at the left and, at the right, the group of the Just who stretch their hands toward Jesus. They come from an edifice and their ancestors lift themselves from a sarcophagus. Behind it, half covered, is the tall crude figure of Hades under the feet of Christ.

Anastasis
Fresco, 10th century

The miniatures of early Psalteries preserve many elements of pre-iconoclast painting. There are good reasons for assuming that they were created in Constantinople. They are still relaxed, free and not dogmatic. Their style is not easily applicable to murals. However, new schemes of composition emerging after 1000 in church art are also prompted by book illumination. Vice versa, in book painting from the tenth century on there is more conformity to compositions on murals. As a result, there is from then on much less discrepancy between miniatures and mural painting.

A similar development may be discerned with respect to ivory reliefs. From the ninth century we have a rather strange anastasis on a little ivory box in the Museum of Stuttgart (see page 29). The main group consists of Christ, Adam and Hades. At each side we see two large sarcophagi, the covers partly removed. Altogether there are eight figures rising from the sarcophagi and stretching their hands toward Christ. They are in no way characterized. The wide low format produces the

Anastasis · Fresco, beginning of the 8th century

Anastasis · Miniature, 9th century

effect that the resurrection of the anonymous dead is much more stressed than is the main group. There is a beautiful quasi-ancient figure of Hades.

Other ivory tableaux, in contrast to the Stuttgart relief, have more in common with tenth century mural painting. Soghanli is an example. An anastasis on a diptych wing in the treasury of the cathedral of Milan is similar. A triptych in the Louvre (see page 31) shows more figures: not less than five behind Adam and Eve and two additional behind the two kings. The triptych wing of Dresden (see page 32) represents an innovation in that St. John the Baptist stands before the two kings and points to Christ. In the Nicodemus gospel John the Baptist had proclaimed the imminent arrival of the Lord. He now awakens hope in the Just dead in Hades where both Satan and Hades had become violently restless as a result of the announcement.

The eleventh century brings about changes. In art works of ivory an entirely new type appears and from then on is used exclusively. Christ no longer steps toward Adam but turns away for He is about to leave Hades and drags Adam along. Christ always carries the cross staff in His left hand. The presence of the Baptist has become obligatory. Already in the Chludow Psalter the emerging Christ had played a role, but here — according to Weitzmann — we are not concerned with the development of an older prototype: this is an innovation of Macedonian Renaissance. The salvation is completed, Christ ascends, followed by Adam. On another ivory fragment in Berlin, Christ ascends in a like manner by stepping over Hades who

Anastasis · Miniature, 9th century

is defeated. That icon shows the back of the Lord, rarely seen otherwise in Byzantine art.

There is no question that the new type of composition makes the moment of Salvation more meaningful than it had been be-

ΒΡΟΤΩΝΑΠΑΡΧΗΝΟΥΡΑΝΟΔΡΟΜΟΝΛΑΒΩΝ

Anastasis · Byzantine, 9th century

fore. However, the reason for the new form lies, on the other
hand, in its direct reference to Antiquity, a reference not infrequent in mid-Byzantine iconography. Hercules was regarded
the victor over the powers of the Netherworld. A London sarcophagus shows him as he leaves the Netherworld with Cerberus
in order to bring him to Mycene in fulfillment of his duties. The
relationship of the emerging Christ with Hercules is evident, and
surely the relationship Hercules/Christ was intentional for the
myths of Antiquity were so firmly planted in Byzantine consciousness that gods and heroes of Hellas were just as easily
used as models and witnesses of Christ as were the prophets of
the Old Testament.

Nor is the new type limited to ivory art. It is found likewise
on murals and in book illuminations. Its oldest representation
(see page 35) is from the eleventh century and is found in the
monastery church of Hosios Loukas. We see Christ above the

cave of the Underworld and we see doors, keys and locks, but not Hades. Christ holds Adam's wrist with His left hand and drags him along. The *protoplasts* stand or kneel before the sarcophagus, which is highly ornamented. At the left there are David and Solomon, also in a sarcophagus. Christ carries a large cross in His right hand. The composition is severe, symmetrical and ancient in its simplicity. The dramatic impact is subdued. Only the end of Christ's mantle represents agitated movement. A golden background filling the total area engulfs all figures and increases the solemnity and sacredness of everything depicted. The artist by reducing the composition and by emphasis upon statue-like representation of all personages obtains a most impressive effect. This is not as much the victor who has overcome Hades, as it is the image of a triumphant Christ who, as the Redeemer, far excells the heights of the other personages who seem almost to be his assistants. The new thought is more purposefully expressed in the miniature of the Codex Iwiron (see page 36) which is clearly divided into two areas. The lower area delineates the Underworld as a hill on the top of which we see a small figure, the defeated Hades. At the sides of the hill are Adam and Eve lifting their hands to heaven where, in the upper area, Christ appears with outstretched arms in a *mandorla*. At His left side there are the kings, at the right St. John with the Just, at the upper corners the angels. There is no touching of the wrists of the ancestors, a motive which all portrayals thus far and of later times have in common. There is a complete renunciation of the portrayal of a course of action. This is the tribute

Anastasis · Byzantine, 10th century

Anastasis · Byzantine, 10th century

of the redeemed to the Lord, expressed in a scheme reminiscent of metamorphosis.

This "liturgical" form of the anastasis is rare. We find it in a twelfth century example in the National Library of Paris (see page 39). There are eight areas around the main area; in all of them we see winged angels with candles, as well as others who have been redeemed or who may be regarded as assistants. The Codex in question contains the homilies of Gregor of Nazianz, a collection of sermons which, as others of the type, demanded from the illustrator the concordance of his miniatures with the text. The mandate often resulted in deviations from the canon or in additions to the customary prototype. In another collection of this type from the fourteenth century (see page 40) Gregor of Nazianz himself replaces the Baptist, like the Baptist points to Christ and turns toward the regal couple (!) behind Him. A late example of such a "liturgical" anastasis is the Russian icon of the sixteenth century in the Eremitage of Leningrad.

The new type is used also in book illumination, for instance, in a collection of the Lawra Monastery in Athos where two persons are added, as is seen on page 43. One sees behind the kings St. John the Baptist and behind the ancestors a young shepherd, possibly Abel with his shepherd's staff. In the Nicodemus gospel Christ addresses Adam with the words: "Peace be with you and all your sons the just men!" Consequently the group of ancestors was enlarged by Abel and in that manner was balanced with another triumvirate, David, Solomon and St. John. Both groups are surrounded by hills which effect some sort of a scenery, though only a later period developed such paraphernalia to a "Hades landscape." The lower part of the icon beneath the figures depicts the dark entrance to Hell and is covered with all sorts of fragments. In contrast to Hosios Loukas Christ steps toward the right so that the *protoplasts* are in the left half of the icon, which is the common procedure.

In a miniature of an *Evangeliar* in London from the twelfth century the figures are more closely joined and considerably reduced in size when related to the entire area. A high mountain reaches from beneath into the icon and engulfs the cave and its ιarge portals. The figure of Christ conceals in part the upper half of the hill. The *tetra-evangelium* of the public library of Leningrad (gr. 105) shows Christ standing in front of the hill of Hell.

Miniatures of the same type are the *Evangeliar* of Paris Ms. gr. 75 (eleventh century) and the anastasis of Cod. Vat. Urb. gr. 2 (1122) where also angels appear with the tools from the Passion; further the anastasis on the Pala d'oro in San Marco and the enamel on a golden book binding in the library of Siena; the tableau with the twelve festivals in Toledo (twelfth century) and another like it in the monastery Vatopädi (thirteenth to fourteenth century), and a tableau in the Vatican library Mus. Sacro 981.

The bronze-founder Barisano who in the last half of the twelfth century created the portals of cathedrals in Trani, Monreale Nord and Ravello, used an identical Byzantine prototype. A miniature from the thirteenth century, gr. 382 in the Public

Anastasis · Mosaic, beginning of the 11th century

Library of Leningrad, indicates the extent to which this Christ figure had become part of the pictorial association of the mid-Byzantine period. In said miniature Christ with the cross in His left hand is seen over the cave of the Underworld. His right hand is stretched out, no figures surround Him. Job alone appears at the left side at great distance to the Lord. A typical example of Byzantine icon-language, the isolated Christ personifies the answer to Job's complaint (Job 17, 13): "The grave is mine house and I have made my bed in the darkness." In the *Evangeliars* the anastasis is often added to the icon of the Evangelist John, either on a complete page or as a vignette in the ornament of the framework. The combination is based on the fact that the beginning of St. John's gospel is read on Easter Sunday in the orthodox liturgy.

In mural painting the new type becomes the popular and official form of portrayal of the anastasis during the mid-Byzantine period. All territories with Byzantine influence cultivate it, from Russia to Jerusalem, from Cappodocia to Italy. In the middle of the eleventh century the center nave of the Hagia Sophia in Kiev displayed a fresco with an anastasis which, as one can gather from page 44, was of considerable width and remarkable depth.

A pilgrim in 1172 writes of the Tomb Church of Jerusalem: "Our Lord, as shown in the sanctuary penetrates into heaven carrying the cross in His left hand holding Adam by His right. He looks toward heaven, His steps are gigantic, His left foot is raised, His right still on earth." The anastasis could, of course, have filled such a permanent place only in said church, yet the example was imitated later in the Chora church in Constantinople.

And a fresco from the church of Karanlik (see page 47) shows the same type as do other cave monasteries of Cappadocia. Here Christ stands at the entrance to the Netherworld stepping on the crouching Hades. The cross staff, symbol of victory, is set upon the tousled head of the defeated who, turning around, has his tremendous mouth wide open. The painter wants to depict the avidity of death which spares no man. "Pamphagos," which means omnivorous, is the name of Hades in the Nicodemus gospel. One sees in segment the haloes of six persons identified by inscriptions as prophets. On page 48 we see a reproduction of that monumental anastasis on the west wall of the cathedral of Torcello where it is seen above the portrayal of the Last Judgment.

Above the anastasis there is also the Crucifixion. All in all, then, Christ appears on three different levels — on the cross, as the Resurrected, and as the Redeemer. The Resurrected outdoes in size the two other Christ figures even though the anastasis claims considerably less space here then does the Last Judgment. Besides, the anastasis does not cover the complete wall for the two angels Michael and Gabriel, delineating the scene, take more than one-third of the total area. The presence of angels in the anastasis is not exactly uncommon and in fact after the twelfth century is almost the rule, yet here the angels are not integrated into the composition. They are outside of it and face the on-

Anastasis · Miniature, 12th century

† τοῦ ἐν ἁγίοις πρ̅σ̅ ἡμῶν γρηγορίȣ ἀρχιεπι̅σ̅
ναζιανζȣ τοῦ θεολόγȣ. λόγος εἰς
τὸ ἅγιον πάσχα. καὶ εἰς βραδυτῆτα
μιᾶς ἀναστάσεως ἡμέρα. καὶ ἠ ἀρ
χὴ. διΰξιȣ· καὶ λαμπρȣ φωῶ
μῶν τῆ πανηγύρει. καὶ ἄλλη

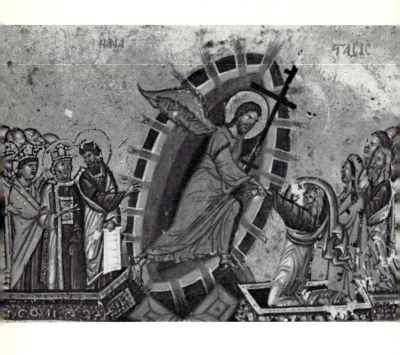

Anastasis · Miniature, 14th century

looker. Probably their function is to reduce the width of the format so as to facilitate the copying of a certain model.

The cave is a semi-circle and similar to the fresco of Karanlik except that Christ here stands on both portals and Hades. At the left we see, behind Adam and Eve, David and Solomon. As in Soghanli, kings rise from a sarcophagus; beneath them there are three little figures vividly gesticulating. They, too, are in a sarcophagus. There is clearly a contrast between the light figures and the dark opening of the cave. On the right side of the picture, too, there are, in the corresponding place, the same figures above which we see a group of prophets who are referred to the event by John the Baptist. The descent, in the composition of Torcello, surprises us by the abundance of figures; altogether seventeen people are visible with others hinted at in the background by means of various haloes. In this respect Torcello is "modern," yet an "archaic" ingredient is implied, too. In order to place all persons the artist has created four different sizes of personages which, in turn, meant resignation of scenic unity, a unity which had been conquered by the eleventh century. As a result, the Torcello mosaic is a succession of pictures, a summarization, one, to be sure, that is not without attractiveness as decoration *per se*.

The emerging Christ in monumental size is seen for the last time at the beginning of the thirteenth century in San Marco of Venice (see page 51). The large mosaic preserves the classical scheme particularly if one disregards the group of four prophets or evaluates them as an invention of the creator of the mosaic.

The artist was a man of the West, as is testified by expressive and dramatic movements, by rhythmically impetuous drapes and folds, by the profile of the head of the prophet and by the peculiar place for Hades which indeed graphically illustrates his defeat. And once more we see Hades reaching out for Adam's foot.

After this San Marco example there are no more monumental compositions of the anastasis belonging to this type. It disappears after a reign for two centuries, and priority is given over to the old manner: Christ's descent into the Netherworld. In two significant mosaics of the mid-Byzantine period, the old prototype had survived, in the middle of the eleventh century in the Nea Moni of Chios, and, at the end of it, in the Daphni monastery near Athens.

The anastasis beneath the great cupola of Nea Moni is in principle not different from the Soghanli fresco, which is about fifty years older. However, while the spaciousness had remained the same, the number of persons had increased by seventeen. They form two well defined groups. The abyss of Hell is symbolized as a semicircle, big, dark and irregular. It resembles Torcello, also with respect to the position of the gates of Hell. In the Chios relic Hades is omitted and Christ is given a large area. And for the first time the vestment of Christ is represented by means of *chrysography*, something hinted at in Hosios Loukas. Here the blue garment is structured by gold stripes and gold flashes of light in concert with the folds of the garment. The Redeemer has unearthly, immaterial stature, and the

Anastasis · Miniature, 11th century

Anastasis · Fresco, middle of the 11th century

splendor of the golden lights is heavenly, a paradisical splendor pushing through darkness. The colorfulness of the mosaic is subdued and shadowy with a prevalence of dark hues, but the figures of the kings and the Just are by no means pale and dead; on the contrary, their garments are replete with saturated colors, and the kings are shown in all their splendor and with regal precious garments ornamented with precious stones. Beneath the dark eyes of solemn faces we see deep shadows.

The Daphni monument (see page 54) seems at first glance of a different prototype, and the only similarity seems the descending Christ. Strangely enough, He is turned to the left. The change is doubtlessly made so that Christ would not walk in the direction of the northern wall. As a consequence, the Redeemer takes Adam with His left hand. This happens only in the Daphni monument except in Hosios Loukas and a few miniatures. The Daphni artist found the classical solution of the theme, and his composition, while concise, is not crowded. Humans rather than objects dominate the scene except for the very large cross that towers over everything. Of a special expressiveness is the juxtaposition of the new and the old Adam. Both have telling eyes. Hades is devoid of all demoniacal traits and his muscular life-size figure is reminiscent of the ancient river god. As later in Torcello, the kings are behind the ancestors and vis-à-vis is St. John with the prophets. This all reminded the connoisseur of Attic reliefs of the classical epoch. There is also the same deep humanity, the same avoidance of dramatic effects, the same atmosphere of directness and dignity. In contrast to Hosios Loukas the action does not address the onlooker but is limited to the theme as represented on the icon. All the elements of miracle and magic are eliminated. This is not an illustration of a dogma of Byzantine theology but a manifestation of the compassion of the Redeemer.

The compositional scheme of Daphni has a model in the miniature, reproduced on page 52, of the Ms. gr. 21 of the Public Library of Leningrad. The icon is from the tenth century. Here, too, Christ turns to the left; here, too, the kings are at the left behind Adam and Eve. The figure of Hades resembles the portrayal from Daphni. At the right side two prophets are seen in profile. They have lifted their hands in prayer. The composition is a direct outgrowth of the old type of Constantinople and differs little from the work in S. Maria Antiqua of Rome. The type had probably been preserved in the Byzantine province. It finds a late reproduction in the Leningrad *Evangeliar* which comes from Trapezunt.

The traditional type of Chios is more frequently found from the twelfth century on. In book illumination it is represented in Cod. sin. 339 and in the *tetra-evangelium* Iwiron 5. From 1191 — see page 60 — dates the impressive fresco in the St. George church in Kurbinowo where the Easter event is portrayed with expressive climaxes, where Christ in hurried steps approaches Adam with the cross on His shoulder bending down to him deeply and lifting him from the grave. Eve's face shows her age, and Abel, astounded, lifts his hand. David and Solomon converse with vivid gestures. Flowing garments effect many folds and cover long body figures.

Anastasis · Fresco, 12th century

Anastasis · Mosaic, 12th century

An eminent artist painted, in ca. 1265, various scenes for the monastery church of Sopočani (see page 56). It was a commission of the Serbian king. Christ here, too, bends deeply over to Adam. The central group is surrounded by many figures. Satan and Hades have been captured by angels at the feet of Christ. In portrayals of that period and of later times this motive is often added until it ultimately becomes a secondary scene, sometimes claiming considerable space. Beneath the prophets there is a large crowd of small figures in white all stretching their hands toward the Redeemer. Specifically added are the two demi-figures of prophets in the upper corners. They hold scrolls in their hands. Since they are not part of the event, they definitely do not belong to the Underworld, nor can they be living personages. They can therefore be identified only with the two people who at the end of the Nicodemus gospel met the redeemed dead at the portals of Paradise and who are asked by them: "Who are you who have not seen death, have not descended to Hell but live in Paradise with body and soul?" And one answered: " I am Henoch who has pleased God and was brought here by Him, and this man here is Elijah." However, Henoch and Elijah were only in exceptional cases integrated into the anastasis. We find them on an icon of Michael Damaskinos and on a tableau from the sixteenth century in the Municipal Museums of Berlin.

The flowering, so-called *palaeologic* epoch, saw a thorough reorientation. Stylistically and iconographically, a new approach meant significant impulses; space is deepened, landscapes are more elaborate, figures are more mobile, scenes are richer, and concentration on light provides more effects. All these and other tendencies characterize the portrayals of the *descensus* in the fourteenth century.

The old Syrian-Palestinian type now is developed to its last and richest form. At the same time there appears a new proto-type at the beginning of the fourteenth century, a synthesis of the Hosios Loukas type and the liturgical anastasis found for instance in Iwiron I. In the latter Codex, but also on a miniature of Vat. gr. 752, Christ stands between Adam and Eve. The synthesis of these types is found for the first time in the apse of a secondary church in Constantinople (see page 59). It is a monumental realization. The place in which the portrayal is found is logical: the church served as a funeral chapel. Christ in white garment with starred *mandorla* takes Adam with His right hand and Eve with His left — on two different sides — and the ancestors seem to escape from the graves. A large number of kings, prophets and other Just is seen on both sides of the center group with large men in elegant vestments. There is a fantastic decor, a rock for background and above a deep blue area. There are delicate and select colors. There are subtle hues. This is a splendor of the greatest delicacy. At the feet of Christ there is the dark entrance to the Netherworld replete with the gates of Hell and fragments of all sorts, and the small brown figure of the captured Hades. However, this fresco of Constantinople, monumental and representative as it is, fascinates us above all because it employs a new manner of composition in which it

Anastasis · Mosaic, beginning of the 13th century

establishes a balance plus an equal value of the two halves of the icon. Naturally the violence of the steps of Christ to which the icon adheres loses, of necessity, its original meaning. Christ is, so to speak, captured by the ancestors, and one can draw no conclusions as to from whence He comes and whither He goes. His vehement step is rendered aimless.

The new type of composition found rapid acceptance. Almost at the same time with the fresco discussed above, there originated that of the Milutin church in Studenica (see page 63), a rich and vivid composition with magnificent figures in a rocky landscape. The end of Christ's garment is thrust upward, as it were, by Christ's violent movement. A little angel in the background holds the cross. This type of composition is cultivated particularly by the Athos monasteries. It appears also in the Northern apses of such monastery churches as Lawra, Dionisiou and Dochiariou (all of the sixteenth century) or in Chilandari (early fourteenth century). In contrast, the motive is strangely varied in Vatopädi where Christ, to be sure, takes both Adam and Eve by His hand but where His figure is forced into a complicated and peculiar posture (because the ancestors are both at the left side of the picture).

The icon from Pskow in the Museum of Leningrad dating from the fourteenth century is symmetrically more severe and indicates the early arrival of the new type in Russia.

In the late Byzantine time the Syrian-Palestinian type is represented once more in portrayals of an especially high quality. We name particularly the mosaic of the Apostle church of Sa-

lonika. It originated in 1312 and is almost contemporaneous with the paintings of the Karije Djami in Constantinople. Though heavily damaged, the Salonika mosaic can stand comparison with the Constantinople works. As the reproduction on page 66 shows, the anastasis is thoroughly classical in its composition and figures. Though there is no dramatization of the event there is, on the other hand, no rigidity. Even the golden garment of Christ does not conceal the well-built body. The physical outlines of the other figures, too, are fully recognizable. The garments and folds of the Just are rendered with pale hues and fine shadows and are delicate in general, and delicate are the heads including the abundant hair of head and beard.

Another product of the fourteenth century is the fresco, shown on page 57, in the Protaton of Athos created by Panselinos. This artist continues the dramatically grouped, spacious scenes previously seen in Kurbinowo and Sopočani. The painter prefers details, width and strong accents. Adam's face is seen in profile. His body is seen as a three-quarter back. A rocky landscape serves as background. The same thought in reduced size is the basis of the little scene of the mosaic icon of Florence pictured on page 58, Christ bends downward but His mantle flows almost vertically upward even more violently than in Studenica. The posture of Christ's body is in tune with that of Adam. Behind Adam we see Eve and Abel, the latter also in profile. The corresponding group on the other side shows David, Solomon and John the Baptist. The blue and black abyss of the

Anastasis · Fresco, ca. 1265

Anastasis · Fresco, 14th century

Netherworld fills the lower half of the icon, but the rock formation of the upper half is in varied reds.

The more frequent appearance of profiles reflects realistic tendencies. Objects are captured with greater accuracy. Late Byzantine painting is in steady quest for original formulations.

Anastasis · Byzantine, 14th century

Not only details but whole schemes of compositions are attempted, and the introduction of or stress on side actions play a great role. Angels can become, instead of accompanying figures, bearers of action. In one of the churches of Mistras, angels hold the defeated Hades captive. In post-Byzantine times this addition is not infrequent.

Anastasis · Fresco, beginning of the 14th century

Anastasis · Fresco, 1191

The extraordinary anastasis from the fourteenth century in the Hodegetria church of Peć, pictured on page 70, has for its core the redemption of the ancestors and of Abel. It is in the upper half of this large, oblong icon. As in Vatopädi Christ seizes Adam and Eve, who are both at the left, but as on the Florentine mosaic icon, Christ bends down to them. Two scenes fill the lower half of the icon: at the right Hades is captured by the two large angels, at the left the Baptist proclaims redemption to the Just in Hades. While the episode had been hinted at only through a gesture of St. John, it is here separated from the chief event so that the total composition becomes a sequence of describing pictures. This manner is in sharpest contrast to the symbolically abbreviated portrayals of Hosios Loukas and Iwiron I. Still another episode is seen on the fifteenth century icon in Leningrad (see page 61). In the cave there are Hades and Satan. They converse. This, too, refers to the Nicodemus gospel. When John the Baptist enters the Netherworld proclaiming

Christ's arrival, the two lords of darkness begin to quarrel: how can one ward off the menacing events? The detail is represented also on an icon of the late sixteenth century in the Benaki Museum of Athens.

Satan and Hades
Byzantine, 15th century

In post-Byzantine times the portrayal of the *descensus* is often thoroughly altered, as a result of the invasion of Western iconography. True — portrayals limiting themselves to the chief figures continue (see page 2), yet many icons show the *descensus* together with the Resurrection from the grave. An example is offered by the Russian icon of the sixteenth century, pictured on page 69, in the Icon Museum of Recklinghausen. Here the sleeping warriors are seen. Models for Russian icons of the seventeenth and eighteenth centuries add to such thematic variation (see page 68). Christ is seen twice in the *mandorla* in one and the same vertical axis. He ascends from the grave around which the sleeping guardians lie, and in the lower part of the picture we see the theme proper, the *descensus*. Behind the *mandorla* with Christ, the elected, accompanied by angels, ascend to the portals of Paradise guarded by a Cherub. Before the door at the helm of the group we see a poor wretch. His figure is seen once more in the Paradise garden where he is welcomed by Abraham and Jacob.

The expansion of the old compositional scheme by similar episodes or by the incorporation of unrelated iconographic details constituted also a danger, to be sure. Critical icon painters and patrons were well aware of it. No wonder, then, that some of the best works of late Byzantine icon painting intentionally retain the genuine, old forms. The icon of Michael Damaskinos (see pages 64/65) in the Benaki Museum of Athens is based on

Anastasis · Fresco, ca. 1314

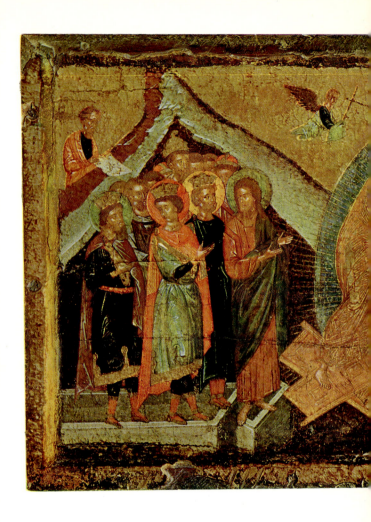

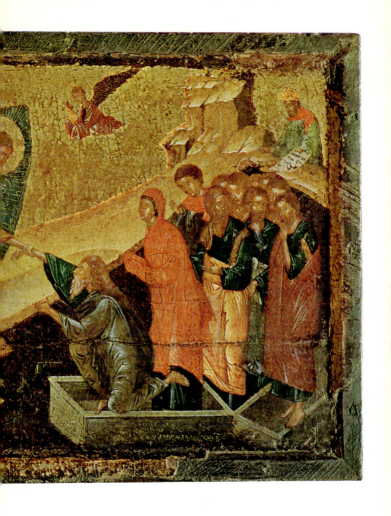

Anastasis · Greek, 2nd half of the 16th century

Anastasis · Mosaic, ca. 1312

prototypes as we found on the mosaic of the Apostle church in Salonika, and, as in Salonika, there are many figures, though here they are rigid at the right as well as at the left, and each group forms an entity. Christ and Adam in the center are completely conventional. The element of the landscape is under-played. The coloristic element is highly intensified. Warm golden-brown, orange, purple and other red hues highlighted by delicate lights contrast with the light blue of the *mandorla* and the pale green in some of the robes. These transparent colors break through the radiant gold of the background. Economy governs the lights and shades of the faces, and these faces seem veiled by fine mist. The glimmer is intensified by the strange deep purple of cave and of undergarments. The icon is indeed a *chef d'œuvre*, a jewel considerably above the *niveau* of most post-Byzantine icons.

The iconography of the descent of Christ has ancient my-thology for its basis. It can serve as an example for the fact that ancient thought and form continue in Christian Byzantine art. To propagate Christian doctrine, Byzantine art leaned on ancient expression. It therefore had the capacity convincingly to represent myth and the supernatural. Hope for salvation is a basic human sentiment which had found expression in ancient times. The Byzantine artist when portraying the descent to Hell could utilize such ancient forms as blueprints, and they would lend validity to his new pictorial statements: he needed not

Anastasis · Russian, 17th century

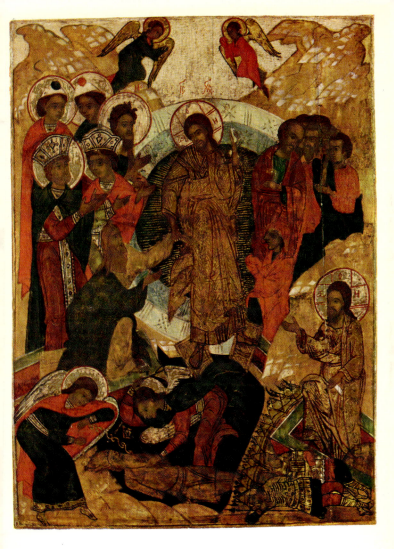

Anastasis · Russian icon, 16th century

confine himself to theology or dogma, however; relying on pre-Christian formulations, he could generalize the theological aspects in terms that were human and universal. One should not denigrate him for his reliance on famous prototypes and for his unwillingness to sever connection with them. We must credit the Byzantine creators for their steady consciousness of the great and unique prototypes and for their ability to refrain from mere imitation.

LIST OF ILLUSTRATIONS